Managing Information

IN1

COMMUNICATING

Published for
The National Examining Board for Supervisory Management

by
Pergamon Open Learning
a division of
Pergamon Press Ltd
Oxford · New York · Seoul · Tokyo

U.K.	Pergamon Press Ltd, Headington Hill Hall, Oxford OX3 0BW, England
U.S.A.	Pergamon Press Inc, Maxwell House, Fairview Park, Elmsford, New York 10523, USA
KOREA	Pergamon Press Korea, KPO Box 315, Seoul 110-603, Korea
JAPAN	Pergamon Press, 8th Floor, Matsuoka Central Building, 1-7-1 Nishi-Shinjuku, Shinjuku-ku, Tokyo 160, Japan

This unit supersedes the Super Series first edition unit 300 (first edition 1985)

Second edition 1991
Reprinted 1992

A catalogue record for this book is available from the British Library

ISBN book and cassette kit: 0-08-041566-0

The views expressed in this work are those of the authors and do not necessarily reflect those of the National Examining Board for Supervisory Management or of the publisher.

Original text produced in conjunction with the Northern Regional Management Centre under an Open Tech Contract with the Manpower Services Commission.

Design and Production: Pergamon Open Learning

NEBSM Project Manager: Pam Sear
Author: Jan Whitehead
First Edition Author: Steven Lane
Editor: Diana Thomas
Series Editor: Diana Thomas

Typeset by BPCC Techset Ltd, Exeter
Printed in Great Britain by BPCC Wheatons Ltd, Exeter

CONTENTS

1   Welcome to the User Guide

Hello and welcome to the NEBSM Super Series second edition (Super Series 2) flexible training programme.

It is quite likely that you are a supervisor, a team leader, an assistant manager, a foreman, a section head, a first-line or a junior manager and have people working under you. The Super Series programme is ideal for all, whatever the job title, who are on or near that first rung of the management ladder. By choosing this programme we believe that you have made exactly the right decision when it comes to meeting your own needs and those of your organization.

The purpose of this guide is to help you gain the maximum benefit both from this particular workbook and audio cassette and also from a full supervisory management training programme.

You should read the whole of this User Guide thoroughly before you start any work on the unit and use the information and advice to help plan your studies.

If you are new to the idea of studying or training by yourself or have never before worked with a tutor or trainer on an individual basis, you should pay particular attention to the section below about Open Learning and tutorial support.

If you are a trainer or tutor evaluating this material for use with prospective students or clients, we think you will also find the information given here useful as it will help you to prepare and conduct individual pre-course counselling and group briefing sessions.

2   Your Open Learning Programme

What do we mean by 'Open Learning'?

Let's start by looking at what is meant by 'Open Learning' and how it could affect the way you approach your studies.

Open Learning is a term used to describe a method of training where you, the learner, make most of the decisions about *how*, *when* and *where* you do your learning. To make this possible you need to have available material, written or prepared in a special way (such as this book and audio cassette) and then have access to Open Learning centres that have been set up and prepared to offer guidance and support as and when required.

Undertaking your self-development training by Open Learning allows you to fit in with priorities at work and at home and to build the right level of confidence and independence needed for success, even though at first it may take you a little while to establish a proper routine.

The workbook and audio cassette

Though this guide is mainly aimed at you as a first time user, it is possible that you are already familiar with the earlier editions of the Super Series. If that is the case, you should know that there are quite a few differences in the workbook and audio cassette, some of which were very successfully trialled in the last 12 units of the first edition. Apart from the more noticeable features such as changes in page layouts and more extensive use of colour and graphics, you will find activities, questions and assignments that are more closely related to work and more thought-provoking.

The amount of material on the cassette is, on average, twice the length of older editions and is considerably more integrated with the workbook. In fact, there are so many extras now that are included as standard that the average study time per unit has been increased by almost a third. You will find a useful summary of all workbook and cassette features in the charts below and on page vii.

Whether you are a first time user or not, the first step towards being a successful Open Learner is to be familiar and comfortable with the learning material. It is well worth spending a little of your initial study time scanning the workbook to see how it is structured, what the various sections and features are called and what they are designed to do.

This will save you a lot of time and frustration when you start studying as you will then be able to concentrate on the actual subject matter itself without the need to refer back to what you are supposed to be doing with each part.

At the outset you are assumed to have no prior knowledge or experience of the subject and can expect to be taken logically, step by step from start to finish of the learning programme. To help you take on new ideas and information, and to help you remember and apply them, you will come across many different and challenging self check tasks, activities, quizzes and questions which you should approach seriously and enthusiastically. These features are designed not only to make your learning easier and more interesting but to help you to apply what you are studying to your own work situation in a practical and down-to-earth way.

To help to scan the workbook and cassette properly, and to understand what you find, here is a summary of the main features:

The workbook

If you want:	Refer to:
To see which other Super Series 2 units can also help you with this topic	The Study links
An overview of every part of the workbook and how the book and audio cassette link together	The Unit map
A list of the main knowledge and skill outcomes you will gain from the unit	The Unit objectives
To check on your understanding of the subject and your progress as you work thorough each section	The Activities and Self checks
To test how much you have understood and learned of the whole unit when your studies are complete	The Quick quiz and Action checks
An assessment by a third party for work done and time spent on this unit for purposes of recognition, award or certification	The Unit assessment The Work-based assignment
To put some of the things learned from the unit into practice in your own work situation	The Action plan (where present)

If you want:	Refer to:
To start your study of the unit	The Introduction: Side one
To check your knowledge of the complete unit	The Quick quiz: Side one
To check your ability to apply what you have learned to 'real life' by listening to some situations and deciding what you should do or say	The Action checks: Side two

Managing your learning programme

When you feel you know your way around the material, and in particular appreciate the progress checking and assessment features, the next stage is to put together your own personal study plan and decide how best to study.

These two things are just as important as checking out the material; they are also useful time savers and give you the satisfaction of feeling organized and knowing exactly where you are going and what you are trying to achieve.

You have already chosen your subject (this unit) so you should now decide when you need to finish the unit and how much time you must spend to make sure you reach your target.

To help you to answer these questions, you should know that each workbook and audio cassette will probably take about *eight* to *ten* hours to complete; the variation in time allows for different reading, writing and study speeds and the length and complexity of any one subject.

Don't be concerned if it takes you longer than these average times, especially on your first unit, and always keep in mind that the objective of your training is understanding and applying the learning, not competing in a race.

Experience has shown that each unit is best completed over a two-week period with about *three* to *four* study hours spent on it in each week, and about *one* to *two* hours at each sitting. These times are about right for tackling a new subject and still keeping work and other commitments sensibly in balance.

Using these time guides you should set, and try to keep to, specific times, days, and dates for your study. You should write down what you have decided and keep it visible as a reminder. If you are studying more than one unit, probably as part of a larger training programme, then the compilation of a full, dated plan or schedule becomes even more important and might have to tie in with dates and times set by others, such as a tutor.

The next step is to decide where to study. If you are doing this training in conjunction with your company or organization this might be decided for you as most have quiet areas, training rooms, learning centres, etc., which you will be encouraged to use. If you are working at home, set aside a quiet corner where books and papers can be left and kept together with a comfortable chair and a simple writing surface. You will also need a note pad and access to cassette playing equipment.

When you are finally ready to start studying, presuming that you are feeling confident and organized after your preparations, you should follow the instructions given in the Unit Map and the Unit Objectives pages. These tell you to play the first part of Side one of the audio cassette, a couple of times is a good idea, then follow the cues back to the workbook.

You should then work through each workbook section doing all that is asked of you until you reach the final assessments. Don't forget to keep your eye on the Unit Map as you progress and try to finish each session at a sensible point in the unit, ideally at the end of a complete section or part. You should always start your next session by looking back, for at least ten to fifteen minutes, at the work you did in the previous session.

You are encouraged to retain any reports, work-based assignments or other material produced in conjunction with your work through this unit in case you wish to present these later as evidence for a competency award or accreditation of prior learning.

Help, guidance and tutorial support

The workbook and audio cassette have been designed to be as self-contained as possible, acting as your guide and tutor throughout your studies. However, there are bound to be times when you might not quite understand what the author is saying, or perhaps you don't agree with a certain point. Whatever the reason, we all need help and support from time to time and Open Learners are no exception.

Help during Open Learning study can come in many forms, providing you are prepared to seek it out and use it:

● first of all you could help yourself. Perhaps you are giving up too easily. Go back over it and try again;

● or you could ask your family or friends. Even if they don't understand the subject, the act of discussing it sometimes clarifies things in your own mind;

● then there is your company trainer or superior. If you are training as part of a company scheme, and during work time, then help and support will probably have been arranged for you already. Help and advice under these circumstances are important, especially as they can help you interpret your studies through actual and relevant company examples;

● if you are pursuing this training on your own, you could enlist expert help from a local Open Learning centre or agency. Such organizations exist in considerable numbers throughout the UK, often linked to colleges and other training establishments. The National Examining Board for Supervisory Management (NEBSM or NEBS Management), has several hundred such centres and can provide not only help and support but full assessment and accreditation facilities if you want to pursue a qualification as part of your chosen programme.

The NEBSM Super Series second edition is a selection of workbook and audio cassette packages covering a wide range of supervisory and first line management topics.

Although the individual books and cassettes are completely self-contained and cover single subject areas, each belongs to one of the four modular groups shown. These groups can help you build up your personal development programme as you can easily see which subjects are related. The groups are also important if you undertake any NEBSM national award programme.

Managing Human Resources				
	HR1	Supervising at Work	HR10	Managing Time
	HR2	Supervising with Authority	HR11	Hiring People
	HR3	Team Leading	HR12	Interviewing
	HR4	Delegation	HR13	Training Plans
	HR5	Workteams	HR14	Training Sessions
	HR6	Motivating People	HR15	Industrial Relations
	HR7	Leading Change	HR16	Employment and the Law
	HR8	Personnel in Action	HR17	Equality at Work
	HR9	Performance Appraisal		

Managing Information				
	IN1	Communicating	IN7	Using Statistics
	IN2	Speaking Skills	IN8	Presenting Figures
	IN3	Orders and Instructions	IN9	Introduction to Information Technology
	IN4	Meetings		
	IN5	Writing Skills	IN10	Computers and Communication Systems
	IN6	Project Preparation		

Managing Financial Resources				
	FR1	Accounting for Money	FR4	Pay Systems
	FR2	Control via Budgets	FR5	Security
	FR3	Controlling Costs		

Managing Products and Services				
	PS1	Controlling Work	PS7	Solving Problems
	PS2	Health and Safety	PS8	Productivity
	PS3	Accident Prevention	PS9	Stock Control Systems
	PS4	Ensuring Quality	PS10	Stores Control
	PS5	Quality Techniques	PS11	Efficiency in the Office
	PS6	Taking Decisions	PS12	Marketing

While the contents have been thoroughly updated, many Super Series 2 titles remain the same as, or very similar to the first edition units. Where, through merger, rewrite or deletion title changes have also been made, this summary should help you. If you are in any doubt please contact Pergamon Open Learning direct.

First Edition

Merged titles
105 Organization Systems and 106 Supervising in the System
100 Needs and Rewards and 101 Enriching Work
502 Discipline and the Law and 508 Supervising and the Law
204 Easy Statistics and 213 Descriptive Statistics
200 Looking at Figures and 202 Using Graphs
210 Computers and 303 Communication Systems

402 Cost Reduction and 405 Cost Centres
203 Method Study and 208 Value Analysis

Major title changes
209 Quality Circles
205 Quality Control

Deleted titles
406 National Economy/410 Single European Market

Second Edition

HR1   Supervising at Work
HR6   Motivating People
HR16 Employment and the Law
IN7   Using Statistics
IN8   Presenting Figures
IN10 Computers and Communication Systems
FR3   Controlling Costs
PS8   Productivity

PS4   Ensuring Quality
PS5   Quality Techniques

The NEBSM Super Series 2 Open Learning material is published by Pergamon Open Learning in conjunction with NEBS Management.

NEBS Management is the largest provider of management education, training courses and qualifications in the United Kingdom, operating through over 600 Centres. Many of these Centres offer Open Learning and can provide help to individual students.

Many thousands of students follow the Open Learning route with great success and gain NEBSM or other qualifications.

NEBSM offers qualifications and awards at three levels:

● the NEBSM Introductory Award in Supervisory Management;

● the NEBSM Certificate in Supervisory Management;

● the NEBSM Diploma in Supervisory Management.

The NEBSM Super Series 2 Open Learning material is designed for use at Introductory and Certificate levels.

The *Introductory Award* requires a minimum of 30 hours of study and provides a grounding in the theory and practice of supervisory management. An agreed programme of five NEBSM Super Series 2 units plus a one-day workshop satisfactorily completed can lead to this Award. Pre-approved topic combinations exist for general, industrial and commercial needs. Completed Super Series 2 units can count towards the full NEBSM Certificate.

The *Certificate in Supervisory Management* requires study of up to 25 NEBSM Super Series 2 units and participation in group activity or workshops. The assessment system includes work-based assignments, a case study, a project and an oral interview. The certificate is divided into four modules and each may be completed separately. A *Module Award* can be made on successful completion of each module, and when the full assessments are satisfactorily completed the Certificate is awarded. Students will need to register with a NEBSM Centre in order to enter for an award – NEBSM can advise you.

Students wishing to gain recognition of competence as defined by the Management Charter Initiative (MCI) or National Vocational Qualification (NVQ) lead bodies, will find that Open Learning material provides the necessary knowledge and skills required for this purpose.

Progression

Many successful NEBSM students use their qualifications as stepping stones to other awards, both educational and professional. Recognition is given by a number of bodies for this purpose. Further details about this and other NEBSM matters can be obtained from:

NEBSM Information Officer
The National Examining Board for Supervisory Management
76 Portland Place
London W1N 4AA

competence-based
programmes

Super Series 2 units can be used to provide the necessary underpinning knowledge, skills and understanding that are required to prepare yourself for competence-based assessment.

Working through Super Series 2 units cannot, by itself, provide you with everything you need to enter or be entered for competence assessment. This must come from a combination of skill, experience and knowledge gained both on and off the job. If you wish to pursue an Open Learning route to a competence-based award you are advised to check with NEBSM as to when and where this type of assessment will be available through them, and with MCI at the address below, as to the actual competency units that need to be assessed as these are subject to change.

Management Charter Initiative
Russell Square House
10–12 Russell Square
London
WC1B 5BZ

You will also find many of the 44 Super Series 2 units of use in learning programmes for other National Vocational Qualifications (NVQs) which include elements of supervisory management. Please check with the relevant NVQ lead body for information on units of competence and underlying knowledge, skills and understanding.

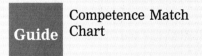

Guide | Competence Match Chart

The Competence Match Chart illustrates which Super Series 2 units provide background vital to the current Management Charter Initiative (MCI) Supervisory sub-set Units of Competence.

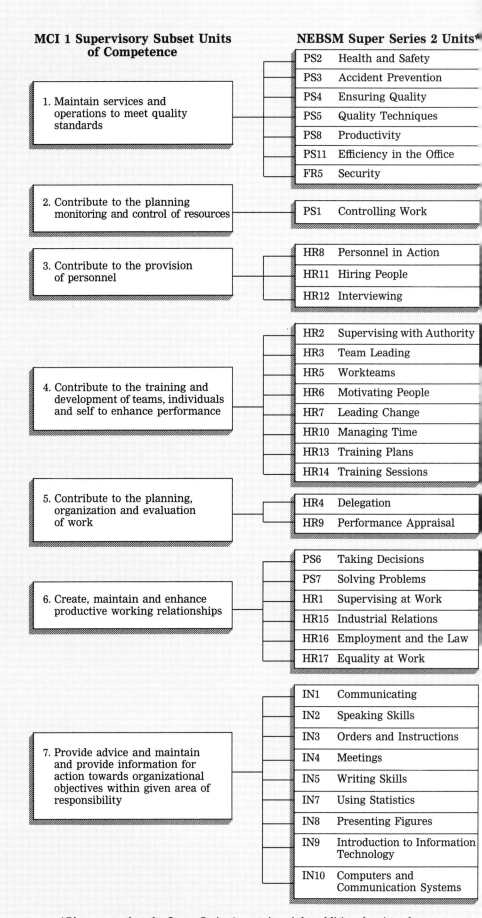

MCI 1 Supervisory Subset Units of Competence

NEBSM Super Series 2 Units*

1. Maintain services and operations to meet quality standards	PS2 Health and Safety
	PS3 Accident Prevention
	PS4 Ensuring Quality
	PS5 Quality Techniques
	PS8 Productivity
	PS11 Efficiency in the Office
	FR5 Security

| 2. Contribute to the planning monitoring and control of resources | PS1 Controlling Work |

3. Contribute to the provision of personnel	HR8 Personnel in Action
	HR11 Hiring People
	HR12 Interviewing

4. Contribute to the training and development of teams, individuals and self to enhance performance	HR2 Supervising with Authority
	HR3 Team Leading
	HR5 Workteams
	HR6 Motivating People
	HR7 Leading Change
	HR10 Managing Time
	HR13 Training Plans
	HR14 Training Sessions

| 5. Contribute to the planning, organization and evaluation of work | HR4 Delegation |
| | HR9 Performance Appraisal |

6. Create, maintain and enhance productive working relationships	PS6 Taking Decisions
	PS7 Solving Problems
	HR1 Supervising at Work
	HR15 Industrial Relations
	HR16 Employment and the Law
	HR17 Equality at Work

7. Provide advice and maintain and provide information for action towards organizational objectives within given area of responsibility	IN1 Communicating
	IN2 Speaking Skills
	IN3 Orders and Instructions
	IN4 Meetings
	IN5 Writing Skills
	IN7 Using Statistics
	IN8 Presenting Figures
	IN9 Introduction to Information Technology
	IN10 Computers and Communication Systems

Please note that the Super Series 2 contains eight additional units relevant to supervisory management (see page ix).

Completion of this Certificate by an authorized and qualified person indicates that you have worked through all parts of this unit and completed all assessments. If you are studying this unit as part of a certificated programme, or think you may wish to in future, then completion of this Certificate is particularly important as it may be used for exemptions, credit accumulation or Accreditation of Prior Learning (APL). Full details can be obtained from NEBSM.

NEBSM SUPER SERIES Second Edition

IN1

Communicating

. . . .

has satisfactorily completed this unit.

Name of Signatory. . . . .
Position. . . . .
Signature. . . . .

Date . . . .

Official Stamp

Pergamon Open Learning and NEBS Management are always happy to hear of your experiences of using the Super Series to help improve supervisory and managerial effectiveness. This will assist us with continuous product improvement, and novel approaches and success stories may be included in promotional information to illustrate to others what can be done.

Guide

1   NEBSM Super Series 2 study links

Here are the Super Series 2 units which link with *Communicating*. You may find this useful when you are putting together your study programme but you should bear in mind that:

● each Super Series 2 unit stands alone and does not depend upon being used in conjunction with any other unit;

● Super Series 2 units can be used in any order which suits your learning needs.

INTERVIEWING
How to plan and carry out this important communication task

SPEAKING SKILLS
How to put your message across clearly and effectively from everyday discussions to formal presentations.

COMPUTERS AND COMMUNICATION SYSTEMS
Communicating by hardware and software needs to be effective too. This unit shows you how.

COMMUNICATING
The principles and practice of effective communication in order to achieve the desired results.

ORDERS AND INSTRUCTIONS
Shows how to tell the workteam what to do in a way that achieves the best results.

WRITING SKILLS
Writing clearly and effectively is an extremely useful communications skill.

MEETINGS
How to plan for and contribute to meetings whether you are leading or are one of the group.

CASSETTE

WORKBOOK

ACTION PLAN

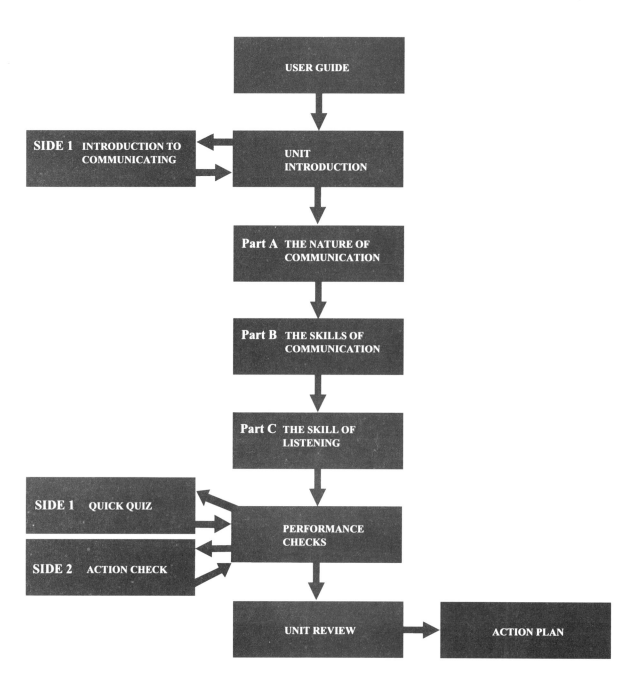

USER GUIDE

SIDE 1 INTRODUCTION TO COMMUNICATING

UNIT INTRODUCTION

Part A THE NATURE OF COMMUNICATION

Part B THE SKILLS OF COMMUNICATION

Part C THE SKILL OF LISTENING

SIDE 1 QUICK QUIZ

SIDE 2 ACTION CHECK

PERFORMANCE CHECKS

UNIT REVIEW

ACTION PLAN

You are largely responsible for the behaviour and productivity of your workteam. So whatever your job involves, you will achieve results through communicating.

This unit shows that this seemingly simple activity which we undertake every day deserves our attention as much as any other aspect of supervision. Good communication means being effective at translating ideas into a message which can be understood correctly by another person and then acted upon. It also means being an attentive listener so that you can interpret other people's messages accurately.

In this unit we will:

● work out why communication is so important;

● think about what is involved in the communication process;

● look at how to plan communications;

● examine the actual skills involved in communicating effectively in speech and writing, in the way we behave and in listening.

Before you start work on this unit, listen carefully to Side one of the audio cassette, which sets the scene for your examination of communicating.

Objectives

When you have worked through this unit you will be ***better able to***:

● identify the benefits to you of being a good communicator;

● design your communication to achieve the results you want;

● communicate more effectively in speech, writing and behaviour;

● listen effectively.

THE NATURE OF COMMUNICATION

1   Introduction

Whether you supervise the day-to-day work of other people in an office, leisure centre, bank, hotel, foundry or assembly shop, you will have one job characteristic in common with every other supervisor – you need to be able to communicate well to manage the activities of your work group. Communication is an essential supervisory skill.

> We must communicate to manage.

Extension 1 The vital role that communicating plays in the job of a supervisor is shown in the Open College video *In charge*. Programme 1 looks at the skills needed to be an effective supervisor in today's workplace.

In this part we will start by defining the term and deciding why communication is so important to achieving our objectives as supervisors. Then we will think about the basic communication skills we all use. We will go on to look at a simple model of the communication process and at some of the ways of putting the model into practice. Finally, there are some basic principles for planning your communication.

2   The importance of good communication at work

Let's start by producing a working definition of this commonly used word 'communication'. It is only when we understand fully what communication involves that we can start thinking about improving our skills.

Activity 1

■ Time guide 8 minutes

Think about the word 'communication' and what it means to you. Look up the word in a good dictionary, if you wish. Then jot down a sentence or two which describes fully what the word means.

_____

_____

_____

_____

If you don't look 'communication' up in a dictionary your definition might be similar to these two below:

■ 'saying something to somebody';

■ 'making yourself understood'.

If you do look the word up, you will find a phrase similar to the following:

■ 'the transfer of ideas between two people';

■ 'the exchange of information';

■ 'the passing of instructions between people which results in action'.

These phrases make some valuable points about the nature of communication:

● it involves a sender and one or more receivers;

● a message is transferred from one to the other;

● it is a two-way process because the transfer of the message results in some kind of response.

You will find many descriptions to choose from, each one with its own merits; however a good working definition which we will use in this unit is:

> Communication is the transfer of information from one person to another, resulting in action.

Communication is rightly regarded by employers as an essential part of a supervisor's job. Let's think about what happens when we fail to communicate.

Activity 2

■ Time guide 5 minutes

If you failed to give instructions to your work group about how to carry out a task which was new to them, what do you think would be the result? Write down *two* outcomes which might result.

_____

_____

_____

_____

Here's my list of points – you may well have thought of more.

■ No one would carry out the task at all.

■ The task would be done badly.

■ Each individual would carry out the task in the way he or she thought was suitable.

Any of these results would mean that you would not be able to achieve your own work group objectives and it would be harmful to your group's productivity and to their morale.

Communication may serve a wide range of work purposes. We need to communicate to:

● instruct;

● inform;

● persuade, encourage or suggest;

● discipline;

● consult or negotiate.

We communicate with management, members of our work group and other supervisors to ensure that our ideas and information are received, understood and acted upon by others.

> Communication brings the minds and actions of people
> closer together to achieve objectives.

If, when you have worked through this unit, you would like to know more about why we need to communicate, you will find this extension helpful and very readable.

Now we have decided why we communicate, let's move on to look at the skills we need.

3   The basic skills

In your daily supervisory duties there are a number of skills you may use when communicating. These can be classified simply as follows.

● Speaking
  You communicate by talking to people face-to-face or on the telephone.

● Writing
  You communicate in writing (whether on paper or screen); this may involve writing letters, memos and reports.

● Behaving
  You communicate by what you actually do and how you look.

There is a further communication skill you use when you are receiving communication from others.

● Listening
  Listening to what others are saying is an essential part of the communication process.

You will probably find that you use a number of these skills together in the duties you undertake. The next activity should help you to recognize the main communication skills involved in some typical supervisory activities.

Activity 3

■ Time guide 8 minutes

We have shown eight typical duties undertaken by supervisors. In each case tick the appropriate column for the main communication skills you would use when carrying out that duty.

	Speaking	Writing	Behaving	Listening
Giving orders to workteam members				
Reporting progress to management				
Receiving suggestions from your workgroup for ways of improving work methods				
Filling in forms and work logs				
Maintaining fair discipline				
Meeting with other supervisors				
Giving training to new staff				
Dealing with problems and grievances				

You will find my choice below with a brief explanation. Your choice may have been slightly different. Differences are not too important at this stage as the main purpose of the activity was to encourage you to think about the communication skills you actually use for specific duties and to show that you use the full range of skills within your own job.

■ Giving orders to workteam members.

  Speaking – *This helps you to determine immediately whether they have understood.*

■ Reporting progress to management.

  Writing – *Writing provides a permanent record but there may be many occasions when oral reporting [speaking] would be appropriate.*

■ Receiving suggestions from your work group.

  Listening *followed by* ***behaving*** – *You need to demonstrate that you are willing to consider their views and you need to act on some of their suggestions if you want them to keep contributing.*

■ Filling in forms and work logs.

  Writing – *There is no other way of carrying out this duty!*

- Maintaining fair discipline.

  Behaving *– This is the best way to show that you are fair.*

- Meeting with other supervisors.

  Speaking *and* ***listening*** *– You need to divide your time between the two skills.*

- Giving training to new staff.

  Speaking *and* ***behaving*** *– Training usually involves explanation and demonstration. In some cases written reference material may need to be provided as well.*

- Dealing with problems and grievances.

  Listening *followed by* ***behaving*** *– You need to fully understand the nature of the problem and it would probably require some action on your part to resolve it.*

Whatever particular skills you are using, there is a basic process involved in all communication. We will look at this process next.

4   The communication process: a model

You remember that our earlier definition of communicating was 'the transfer of information from one person to another, resulting in action', so it has these main elements.

- Information
  We communicate because we want to convey information.
- People
  People are involved both as senders and as receivers of information.
- Action
  The purpose of conveying the information is to achieve a specific result.

We can convert these three features into a simple model, which represents the communication process.

Let's look at each of the features of the process in turn.

**4.1
Information**

Information is the substance of communication and is sometimes referred to as the message. It is ***what*** we want to say. You always need to be very clear about the substance of any communication at the outset.

We can use the case in the following activity to show the difference between the substance of communication and the way it is transmitted.

Activity 4

■ Time guide 5 minutes

Jane Mansell is the supervisor in a section which enters insurance information onto computer files. She walks into the office one morning and finds Timothy Powell, an operator, drinking coffee at his terminal despite an instruction issued by Jane that this is not allowed.

What is the substance of the information Jane needs to convey to Tim?

_____

_____

If you were in Jane's place, what words would you use to convey the information to Tim?

_____

_____

_____

I think you'll agree that the substance of Jane's information is that refreshments should not be drunk at terminals. However, there are many ways she could actually convey that message. Three ways are given below.

■ A question
'Why have you disobeyed me by drinking coffee at your terminal, Tim?'

■ An order
'Please take your coffee away from your terminal at once, Tim.'

■ A statement
'I see you've disobeyed my instructions by drinking your coffee at your terminal, Tim.'

You may have your own variations of any of these. This second part of the activity leads us into thinking about the next feature of the communication process: people.

4.2
People

Each time we communicate a message to someone else, **we** (the sender) determine **how** we will communicate with the other person (the receiver). We decide the words we will use; how we will phrase those words and the tone we will use.

Although the communication model is in itself simple, it is often people who make communication an extremely complex process. You will find that there are a number of factors that will affect your own choice of how you communicate. Your approach to communication will reflect:

● your own **personality**: you may be forthright or shy;

● your **feelings** at the time: you may be angry, resentful or happy;

● your **attitude** towards the people with whom you are communicating: you may like or distrust them;

● your **knowledge**: you may know very little or a great deal about what you are communicating;

● your **experience**: you may have previous experience of similar situations.

We can summarize these factors as your **attitudes** and your **experiences**. The same factors will also determine how you respond to information you receive from other people. The following example should help to explain this point.

Case
Study

John works in a large mail order office and is known to his supervisor as being work shy and always ready to complain about anything. Charlene, on the other hand, is a high producer and always ready to co-operate over any work plan changes.

The supervisor has just set some work targets for the use of new equipment and asks John how he is getting on with these targets. John's reply is, 'The target's too high. I may make it for the odd half-hour – there's no way anyone's going to keep up with those targets.'

Charlene's reply is, 'Well, I can't be sure yet, but I'm finding it difficult to stay up with the targets for more than half an hour. I think the others will be in the same boat.'

The substance of the message from John and Charlene is the same. However, the way the supervisor will interpret the message from each of them may be very different.

Most supervisors would use the past experience of John and Charlene, i.e. that one was 'work shy' and the other a 'high producer', to put greater trust in the accuracy of the message received from Charlene.

You will find that we all allow our attitudes and experiences to influence the meaning we give to information. In written communication, we often refer to it as 'reading between the lines'. The substance of the information is frequently the least potent part of the message. It is the context of the message – these other human factors surrounding the message – which are more powerful in determining the way it is interpreted.

How information is presented is more powerful
than what is being said.

Here's another activity which demonstrates this point.

Activity 5

■ Time guide 5 minutes

Think of yourself as a customer on the receiving end of the following communications.

■ A sales assistant in a shop comes up to you slouching, with his head down and says 'Can I help you?' in a bored tone of voice. What message do you actually receive?

_____

_____

■ You receive a promotional letter from a hotel chain stating the efficiency and caring attitude of their staff, but the letter is badly typed, contains spelling mistakes and is unsigned. What message do you actually receive?

_____

_____

If your reaction is the same as mine, the message you actually receive is the opposite from what is said. As a result, the sales assistant is unlikely to make a sale and the hotel is most unlikely to get your custom. So the communication has not resulted in the right *action*.

4.3
Action

This brings us to the third feature of the communication model. All communication has a purpose: it should result in some kind of action. The word 'action' usually conjures up the image of some kind of physical activity which can be observed. Here is an example of what I mean.

- *Information*: 'Go to my office and bring me the file for the Bartons account.'

- *People*: supervisor to clerk.

- *Action*: clerk goes to the office and returns with the file. Sometimes communication results in action which is difficult to observe. Try the following activity.

Activity 6

■ Time guide 4 minutes

A supervisor sends a routine progress report to a manager stating an increase in output for the month from 250 units to 300 units.

What kind of results may there be from this communication that it is impossible to *see*? Jot down *two* suggestions.

_____

_____

_____

_____

Your experiences may differ from mine, but see if you agree with the ideas I jotted down. This transfer of information may result in:

■ adding to the manager's existing knowledge;

■ confirming (or reversing) the manager's existing impression about trends;

■ confirming (or reversing) the manager's attitudes towards the supervisor and the work group.

These results are producing *changes in the manager's way of thinking* rather than observed action. We have already seen that action usually means a change in behaviour but:

changes in the mind are actions too.

So far the model looks deceptively simple. There is a complication which needs to be considered: the existence of *barriers to communication* which prevent the information from being interpreted properly by whoever is receiving it.

We have already covered one barrier to effective communication – the *attitudes* and *experiences* of the receiver. If hostile attitudes exist and there have been poor relationships between sender and receiver arising from previous encounters, any new communication runs the risk of being misinterpreted or ignored.

Activity 7

■ Time guide 6 minutes

Can you think of other barriers that you have encountered which have hindered the actual transmission of information to the receiver? Try to think of at least *three*.

_____

_____

_____

Once you started on this activity I expect you thought of more than three. I have categorized my ideas under some headings.

■ Noise
  Any kind of noise, whether it is machinery, printers, telephones, traffic or people, can make it difficult to hear or concentrate and may cause distortion of a message.

■ Language
  Sometimes the words that are used in communication cause the message to be misinterpreted. This can happen if imprecise words are used, for example 'sort of' or 'things'; also technical jargon can be confusing if it is unfamiliar to the other person. For instance, 'I'll just call up the **data** on my **VDU**.'

■ Environment
  It is possible for people not to receive information properly because aspects of the work environment intervene, such as answering the telephone when someone is by your side trying to hold a conversation at the same time.

■ Authority relationships
  Another barrier to effective communication you have encountered is the pattern of authority relationships in organizations. Sometimes you may feel that communication has to go through some over-complicated systems to reach the right person and that, by the time it reaches them, it has become distorted.

These barriers exist for all of us. We cannot always remove them but we can recognize the effect they have and do our best to reduce their impact.

Extension 2 This important topic is covered very well in Chapter 1 of N. Stanton's *What Do You Mean 'Communication'?* and is well worth reading.

Activity 8

■ Time guide 5 minutes

What could you do to reduce the barriers in the following situations?

■ You sometimes do not hear messages correctly because you are distracted by the noise from printers and telephones in the open plan office in which you work.

_____

_____

_____

■ You are often short-staffed because any request for new staff to fill vacancies is passed up to the departmental head (three levels above you) before it is passed on to Personnel.

_____

_____

_____

I thought of two alternatives for dealing with the first situation.

■ You could investigate what could be done to reduce the noise from the printers and telephones, such as sound-proofing hoods on printers or using light signals rather than ringing tones for telephones.

■ You could try to create a quiet work area by the use of partitioning/sound-proof screens.

I found the second situation more difficult to resolve.

■ You might be tempted to by-pass the formal system and go straight to Personnel but that would be undermining your management's authority – not a good move!

■ Your could discuss the matter with your manager, explain the problem and find out whether there is a valid reason for having authorization at top departmental level.

These barriers can hinder the transmission of information. However, in order for the communication process to be complete we must be sure that the receiver fully understands the message and will respond in a positive way. Let's look at that next.

Often we think we have completed the communication process when we have given the other person the information. This means that we are assuming that it will lead to action. We can see the problems that arise from making these assumptions in the next activity.

Activity 9

■ Time guide 5 minutes

Atmoprint is a successful firm in the printing industry. They currently have more orders than they can easily cope with. An important rush printing order has just come in. Jean, the supervisor, decides to give this job to Margaret. She takes Margaret to the print room and explains how to operate the machine. She then gives Margaret the details of the order and leaves her to get on with it.

One hour later she realizes Margaret is still in the print room when she should have finished much earlier. Rushing down, Jean discovers that the order is not even half-completed and that Margaret is staring unhappily at the machine, which is not running.

Did Jean follow the communication model:

Information passed between *people* to result in *action*?

_____

What else could Jean have done which would have helped to avoid this problem? Try to think of *two* ways of avoiding this problem.

_____

_____

_____

_____

You may have decided that Jean could avoid this problem by:

■ asking Margaret whether she understood;

■ telling Margaret where she could be found and to come and find her immediately she encountered any problems;

■ staying to watch Margaret, to make sure Margaret was confident in operating the machine.

In fact, Jean neglected to think about two crucial questions which are important in all our communications.

● How do we know the other person *understands* the information?

● How can we be confident that the right *action* will result?

If we want to communicate effectively, we cannot leave the answers to these questions to chance. We must obtain some kind of message back from the receiver that our information has been fully understood. The term used for this is 'feedback'. We can now insert this into the communication model.

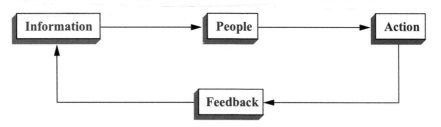

You remember that we said earlier that we can identify two kinds of feedback from receivers. These are:

● Feedback by action;

● Feedback from the person.

If Jean gets Margaret to demonstrate that she can operate the machine by showing her, then the feedback comes from the action and can be incorporated into the model in the following way.

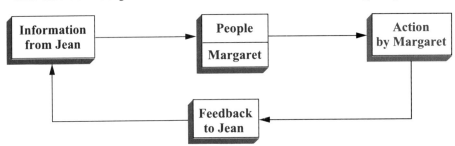

However, if Jean asks Margaret a question about whether she understands, then this is securing feedback from the person and can be shown like this:

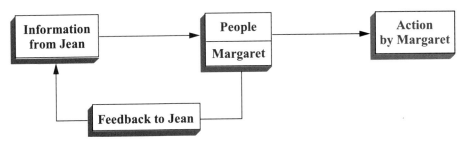

Action feedback is the better way of making sure that communication has been effective. *Person feedback* causes more problems because a person will respond to the question which is asked.

Extension 3 If you would like to know more about this communication model, the short video *A Question of May* is very good at explaining it.

Let's go back to our case example in Activity 9.

Activity 10

■ Time guide 4 minutes

When Jean had finished her explanation of how the machine worked, she could have asked Margaret, 'Do you follow me? Are you clear about what you've got to do?'

Jot down why you think this might be a poor way of obtaining feedback?

_____

_____

_____

Did you recognize that both these questions only allow for a yes or no answer? You are merely getting a statement of what the other person thinks she knows. If you ask these kinds of questions, there may be very good reasons why the receiver gives an inaccurate answer. For example, Margaret may answer 'Yes' to the questions merely because she does not want to appear slow, unintelligent, or incapable in front of her supervisor.

You may have experienced this yourself. Often people prefer to go away and fathom out a difficulty for themselves or to ask someone else after you have gone away. At the best, this wastes time and at the worst it may risk injury, spoilt materials or damaged equipment.

It is far better to ask a question that requires them to 'replay' the instruction. Here are some examples that Jean could have used.

● 'What are the most important points to bear in mind when operating this machine?'

● 'We've looked at how this machine works and you've had a practice. Now, how are you going to tackle this order?'

You can also confirm a person's answers by looking at them and observing the way they behave. Look at their facial expressions and their gestures. Do they look confident and certain or do doubtful expressions cross their faces? Are they nodding or shaking their heads? Are they calm and controlled in their gestures and movement or are they nervous, jumpy and clumsy? You need to ask questions, listen to their replies and look at their reactions to see if they have fully understood and that understanding is likely to lead to action.

You can use these techniques to secure feedback in face-to-face situations but it may be more difficult to secure feedback from people or action when you are using written communication methods. In the next activity you need to think about how you can obtain feedback when you are writing to people.

Activity 11

■ Time guide 5 minutes

When you write a memo or a letter, how can you check whether the receivers have understood and are going to act in the way you want? Write down *two* ways you might achieve this.

_____

_____

_____

_____

Did you experience any difficulty with this activity? Written communication is sometimes referred to as one-way communication because feedback may be delayed or even non-existent. See if your list of ways of securing feedback from written communication is similar to mine. You can:

■ *ask specific questions* so that they have to write or telephone in order to answer the questions;

■ *state clearly the kind of response you want*, for example, you can write, 'Please confirm this appointment by telephone before 25 January 199_' rather than, 'I look forward to hearing from you as soon as possible';

■ *use the last sentence for stating the action you want*, this means that it is the last information they read and therefore they should remember it more easily.

Getting feedback is important but may not always be easy. However:

Feedback helps to ensure that communication
produces the required result.

As in all activities, half the success of effective communication comes from planning.

Extension 2 You will find two useful chapters in N. Stanton's book on preparing communication and planning communication if you want to know more about this topic.

The more thought and effort we put into thinking through our communication in advance, the more likely it is to be successful. The immediate reply that most of us make when challenged about poor communication is, 'I'd communicate more effectively if I had the time to sit back, think and plan – but when does a busy supervisor find time to do this?'

Activity 12

> ■ Time guide 5 minutes
>
> Write down ***three*** of the factors that would influence the amount of time you spend on planning your communications.
>
> Example: the importance of the task
>
> _____
>
> _____
>
> _____

I hope we can agree that some of the most important factors included are:

■ your own knowledge and experience;

■ the other person's knowledge and experience;

■ the seriousness of failing to communicate effectively;

■ how well you knew and got on with the other person;

■ the complexity of the information that needed to be communicated.

You will have to decide how much time you spend on planning each communication, but, whatever time you decide, there are some simple principles to follow in planning any communication. These are to be decided in advance and are listed below.

● ***Why*** you are communicating.

*You need to be clear in your own mind about your **purpose**.*

● ***What*** you are communicating.

*You need to be clear about the **substance** of the information.*

● With ***whom*** you are communicating.

*You need to think what you know about the **receiver** including their knowledge, experience, skills, attitudes and previous relationship to you.*

● ***How*** you should communicate.

*You need to decide the most appropriate **method** of communicating and the way you will present the information.*

In some cases you also need to decide the following.

● ***When*** you should communicate.

You should decide the best time for giving the information.

● ***Where*** you should communicate.

> *Sometimes the substance of the communication may require privacy and quiet or it may be better to discuss a matter off work premises.*

Let's use an example to illustrate these points.

Robbie Dent was a supervisor in a firm manufacturing haulage gear to the mining industry. It was winter and a couple of the men in Robbie's section were off with flu. Robbie noticed a patch of oil across a gangway. As there weren't many men in and the tank section on the gangway wasn't manned that morning, it wasn't an immediate problem but it was a safety hazard and needed to be cleaned up.

He called across to Dougie, a newcomer to the section, who was bent over some work on his bench.

'There's some oil across the gangway up there, Dougie'.

Dougie looked up briefly. 'Aye, could be nasty, that', he agreed.

'That's right,' Robbie said. 'It'll have to be cleaned up'.

Just then Robbie was called over to the offices to sort out order forms. While he was there he received a message that there had been an accident in his section. It was nothing serious, but someone who had arrived late had slipped and sprained his wrist. He'd be off work for a week.

Robbie was furious. The accident had been caused by the oil patch. He went over to Dougie.

'I told you to clean it up!' he said angrily.

'No you didn't!' Dougie replied. 'If you had, I'd have done it'.

You can see that the information Robbie ***thought*** he'd given was not the information Dougie ***thought*** he heard. Let's explore the reasons behind this communications failure by returning to our basic communication model.

■ Information
  The measure is not clear. Is Robbie giving an instruction or is he merely passing on information as a warning? Is it clear what he wants to achieve?

■ People
  Robbie is treating Dougie as an 'old hand' and forgetting he is a newcomer. Perhaps Dougie is being deliberately awkward.

■ Action
  Robbie does not convey in his information that the required action is for Dougie to clean up the oil.

Possibly the worst failure is the following.

■ Feedback
  Robbie does not use any technique to make sure that Dougie has understood his instruction correctly or set any specific time limits for carrying out the action.

Activity 13

■ Time guide 7 minutes

Try using the four-point planning model of **why, what, who, how** to ensure that Robbie's communication is effective.

Why does Robbie need to communicate?

_____

What is Robbie communicating?

_____

With **whom** is Robbie communicating? What do you know about Dougie?

_____

How should Robbie communicate to ensure that Dougie understands the information and takes the appropriate action?

_____

_____

_____

_____

_____

Let's see if your ideas agreed with mine about this.

■ **Why**: Robbie needs to give an **instruction** to have the oil cleaned up so as to ensure a safe working environment.

■ **What**: The information that needs to be conveyed is:

– the danger of the oil;
– the need to have it cleaned up;
– the urgency with which this action should be taken.

■ **Who**: Robbie needs to remember that Dougie is a **newcomer** and should not assume knowledge that Dougie may not possess.

■ **How**: Robbie should **call Dougie over** to the patch of oil in order to focus his attention on the matter. He should **ask him a question** about the cleaning to make sure that Dougie has understood the instruction and knows where to get the cleaning materials. He should **set a deadline** for the action so that Dougie appreciates that action should be taken quickly.

Communication planning does not need to be a lengthy process each time. However, conscious decisions about **why, what, who** and **how** do need to be made. Remember:

a moment's planning can prove to be very
worthwhile in achieving results.

■ Time guide 5 minutes

Complete the following sentences with a suitable word or words.

1. The communication model has three key features; these are _____ , _____ and action.

2. Feedback can come from action and from _____ .

3. Action can involve a change of _____ as well as a change of behaviour.

4. Our four-point planning model for communication asks what, why, _____ and _____ .

Which of the following statements are TRUE and which are FALSE?

5. Information is the substance of communication. TRUE/FALSE

6. Feedback is additional to the communication process. TRUE/FALSE

7. Our attitudes and experiences affect the way we communicate. TRUE/FALSE

8. All communication needs to be planned. TRUE/FALSE

Response check 1

1. The communication model has three key features; these are: INFORMATION, PEOPLE and action.

2. Feedback can come from action and from PEOPLE (or a person).

3. Action can involve a change of MIND (or thinking) as well as a change of behaviour.

4. Our four-point planning method asks what, why, WHO and HOW.

5. Information is the substance of communication. This is TRUE.

6. Feedback is additional to the communication process. This is FALSE. Feedback is an essential part of the process. You cannot know whether you have conveyed the information correctly in order to achieve results unless you have person or action feedback.

7. Our attitudes and experiences affect the way we communicate. This is TRUE.

8. All communication needs to be planned. This is TRUE.

The purpose of communication is:

● to bring the minds and actions of people closer together.

The basic skills of communicating are:

● speaking;

● writing;

● behaving;

● listening.

A model of the communication process is:

where

● *information* is the **substance** of the communication;

● *people* act as senders and receivers and are affected by *past experiences* and *attitudes*;

● *action* is what we *do* and also what we *think*.

Feedback comes from two sources:

● from the action itself – *action feedback*;

● from the person – *person feedback*.

Communication planning involves thinking in advance about the following.

● *Why?* Why do I need to communicate?

● *What?* What do I want to say?

● *Who?* With whom am I communicating?

● *How?* How do I convey the message to ensure action?

THE SKILLS OF COMMUNICATING

1 Introduction

Now that we have explored the nature of communication, let's move on to developing the basic skills. In this part of the unit we will look at some simple general principles for writing or speaking. After we've compared the advantages of these two methods of communicating, we will consider the skills of writing and speaking in more detail. We will finish by examining communication through the way we look and behave.

2 The basic principles

We often find it easier when developing skills to have a few simple principles we can apply. This is true of communication skills. There are a couple of ways of helping to remember key principles of writing or speaking.

The first method is known as the ABC of communication. This stands for:

Accuracy

Brevity

Clarity

- Accuracy
  Information used at work must be accurate. For example, it's no good asking a customer to pick up goods at 4.00 p.m. if they will not be ready until 5.00 p.m.

- Brevity
  People want relevant, essential information – not a lot of irrelevant, time-consuming extras.

- Clarity
  The message must be clear. If it is vague or can be interpreted in two or three different ways, it will not produce the correct action. An example of a vague, ambiguous message is: 'I think that order number 83711 is needed by lunchtime Thursday.'

Activity 14

■ Time guide 8 minutes

Look at the example we've just given about order number 83711. Work out why it's vague and ambiguous and then rewrite it so that the information is clear.

You could write it many ways but I hope you will agree that the following version eliminates all doubt.

■ Order number 83711 will be completed and ready for delivery by 12.00 noon on Thursday 8 February 199_.

Another way of remembering the characteristics of good communication skills is to think of the five C's of communication. These are that any communication should be:

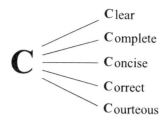

- Clear
The message must be clear so that there is only one possible meaning.

- Complete
When you are writing or speaking you must include *all the information* that is needed to enable the appropriate action to be taken. We can often provide incomplete messages by omitting important points such as dates, times, names or amounts. Incomplete messages left on answering machines are good examples of how failure to observe this principle can frustrate receivers!

- Concise
This means more than being brief. If you are so brief that you do not convey all the information needed, this is not good communication. Concise means *brief but including all the relevant information.*

- Correct
It is essential that the information given is correct.

- Courteous
Since you want some positive action to result from your communication, it is important that you maintain common courtesy and show respect for another person, whatever their level of authority may be within the organization. For example, people do not respond well to an instruction which starts 'Hey, you over there......' Generally the principle is – *treat other people the way you would like to be treated!*

Now let's think about these principles in relation to writing and speaking skills.

3   Methods of communicating

Before looking at specific skills, we'll pause for a minute to compare the advantages of written and spoken communication.

Extension 4 If you would like to carry your examination of different methods of communication further, you will find Chapter 6 of E. Eyre's book *Business Communication Made Simple* very helpful.

On many occasions within your working week you may be faced with a choice.

- Should I telephone a customer or write?

- Should I send a message by memo or go and talk to the person?

Part of the success of communication depends on selecting the right method to meet the needs of the situation. We have given an example in the activity below.

Activity 15

■ Time guide 5 minutes

Mary is the senior ledger clerk in a large accounts department. One Monday morning, a departmental manager wanted some detailed sales figures for a meeting the following week. Mary decided to dictate these figures to him over the telephone.

Do you think this method of communicating was appropriate?

_____

Write down a reason for your decision.

_____

_____

I thought it was **not** a very appropriate method. Did you agree? My reasons were:

■ complex figures can be easily misheard over the telephone;

■ unless she asks him to read the figure back, Mary has no feedback whether he noted them down correctly;

■ there is no great urgency for the figures – the meeting is the following week. A printed set of figures would not necessarily be more accurate but would be less likely to become inaccurate in transmission.

Both written and spoken methods have their own advantages. You can use your own experience to identify some of these.

Activity 16

■ Time guide 8 minutes

Write down *two* situations in which it has been better to use written communication and *two* situations in which it has better to use spoken communication.

Written communication:

_____

_____

_____

Spoken communication:

_____

_____

_____

You may like to compare your list with mine. I have quoted general rather than specific situations but I expect our lists are similar.

Some of the situations in which *written communication* is better are:

■ when you need a *permanent record* of the information for future reference;

■ when the information is the subject of a *contract* or *agreement* or when you think there may be disagreement arising from the information;

■ when you want the receiver to be able to control the time and place they receive the message;

■ when the information is *confidential*.

Some of the situations in which *spoken communication* is better are:

■ when you want *immediate feedback*;

■ when it is necessary to have an *exchange* of information or ideas;

■ when it is a good idea to be able to use *tone* or *body language* to support the substance of the message;

■ when you think it would be wiser not to have a permanent record.

You will need to think carefully each time which method you should use and weigh up the relative advantages. When you are doing this, it is helpful to think about the following factors.

● Clarity
  Which method enables the information to be conveyed clearly and accurately?

● Speed
  How quickly must the other person receive the message and respond to it?

● Cost effectiveness
  Which method will achieve the desired result at least cost?

● Attitude of receivers
  Which method is likely to be most acceptable to the receivers so that they will provide positive feedback?

Now we have compared the two methods, let's move on to examine writing skills in more detail.

4 Writing skills

You will certainly find that a proportion of your time will be spent writing. You may even complain that your supervisory job involves too much pen-pushing! It is therefore important that you develop writing skills which allow you to achieve the results you want as quickly and easily as possible. Your writing may involve:

● making entries on a variety of *forms*;

● passing on *written messages* from one shift to another;

● taking down *telephone messages* to pass on to your manager or to a member of your workteam;

● making out accident *reports* or progress reports;

● sending *memos* to other people within the organization;

● sending *letters* to customers, clients, suppliers and other people outside the organization.

Before we move into a more detailed exploration of writing skills, there is one important fact to bear in mind; that is, whenever you put pen to paper, you are making a statement about yourself. What you write and how you say it conveys an image of you to someone else.

Every piece of writing projects an image of you.

Activity 17

■ Time guide 8 minutes

If you write letters to people outside your organization, what sort of impression do you think they get of you and your organization from your letters?

_____

_____

Try to identify at least *three* points about your letters which convey this impression.

_____

_____

_____

The impression you may get of other companies from their letters can be that they are inefficient, indifferent and couldn't care less about the customer.

You can convey a good or a bad impression in a letter from:

■ the way you set out the letter on the page – its *layout*;

■ the *sequence* in which you present the information;

■ the actual *words* you use;

■ the accuracy of your *use of English*;

■ the *tone* that is conveyed by the phrasing you use.

These points are also important in other forms of written communication you use inside your organization – memos, messages and reports. The success behind written communication is to keep your reader clearly in your mind when you prepare and write. You do not have the advantage of the feedback part of the communication process immediately, as you do in face-to-face communication, so there are several things that you must anticipate.

● Existing knowledge
  You must decide what the readers already know about the subject.

● Additional information required
  You must decide what additional information your readers need or want to know.

● Vocabulary range
  You must consider the likely vocabulary range used by your readers, including their understanding of technical terms.

● Tone
  You must choose your words and phrases very carefully so that they understand the message and are *willing* to take the action you require. You do not want to create a negative reaction in your readers.

● Sequence and layout
You want to present information in an order which is simple and easy for readers to follow. Likewise, the overall layout needs to attract readers to *want* to read the message.

Activity 18

■ Time guide 6 minutes

Look at the following two versions of a memo sent by Charles Read to Palminder Singh, a manager in another department to whom he has spoken once on the telephone. Decide which is the better memo and note down your reasons.

Version 1

From: Charles

To: Palminder

Thanks for the file and the info. I'll burn the midnight oil on this one and let you know the final figures tomorrow. OK?

Version 2

From: Charles Read
        Senior Bookkeeper

To: Palminder Singh
        Marketing Manager

Date: 25 September 1990

Parker file

Thanks for sending me the Parker file and the additional information. I'll be looking at the contents tonight and will calculate the final costings.

The final figures will be on your desk by 10.30 a.m. tomorrow. If you need them earlier than this, please ring me on extension 308 before 5.00 p.m. today.

Version ___ is better because:

_____

_____

_____

_____

_____

I think Version 2 is better. I've contrasted the two versions in my explanation below.

■ Version 2 provides clear, complete and correct information.

Version 1	Version 2
Does not clearly identify the sender of the memo	Gives the sender's full name and job position
Does not state clearly which file has been received – Palminder could send out many files!	States the name of the file for clear identification
Omits important information from the memo headings, that is, the date and the subject	Gives a date in the memo headings so that there is a clear reference point for words such as 'today' and 'tomorrow'
	Also provides a subject heading so that there is instant recognition of the subject of the memo

■ Version 2 considers the reader of the memo more carefully.

Version 1	Version 2
Uses the expression 'burning the midnight oil' which could confuse Palminder	Uses simple, everyday words
Is over-casual in tone for a supervisor to a manager who is virtually a stranger in another department.	Is more cautious and respectful of the manager's position and attitudes.

The first version runs the risk of Palminder Singh being confused about the message and angry or resentful at the tone. It certainly does not convey a good image of Charles Read.

Therefore, when writing:

> keep your reader in the forefront of your mind.

This will go some way to compensate for the absence of immediate person feedback.

Generally, written communication does give you more time for planning what you want to say and how to say it. It also allows you to check over what you have written before sending it. However, once committed to paper and sent, it is a permanent record – so do make sure it fulfils the basic communication principles.

Extension 4 If you would like to know more about writing skills, particularly about the use of language and tone, you will find Chapter 17 of *Business Communication Made Simple* useful.

In trying to achieve a good writing style, it is very tempting to copy a style from someone else. Sometimes this results in a style which uses long, complicated sentences and outmoded expression. Some common examples are:

'We are in receipt of your esteemed communication . . . ,

'Thanking you for favouring us with your order . . .'

These are reminiscent of a Victorian clerk with a quill pen, so don't be tempted to use them. In other cases, written documents become a number of standardized expressions linked together in sentences – as though produced by an impersonal robot. Your employers may have certain standards they like maintained, but this should still allow you to devise a simple, straightforward style of writing which reflects your own personality.

Devise your own style of writing.

We are very conscious of thinking about language and layout when we are writing. It is sometimes a different matter when we are speaking to people – which is what we'll look at next.

5   Speaking skills

Speaking effectively is a skill just as important as that of writing well.

Extension 4 This section will look at some basic points and, if you want to find out more, Chapter 20 on verbal communication in *Business Communication Made Simple* is well worth reading.

There is a very true saying that goes:

'Engage brain before opening mouth!'

Unfortunately it is something we often forget. We spend so much of our time each day talking to people face-to-face, formally or informally, that we forget that we need to give attention to developing our speaking skills if people are to understand us properly and act on our information.

If you think back to the basic communication model, you will appreciate that you need to be aware of the **action** you want to achieve before you start speaking.

Activity 19

■ Time guide 6 minutes

Think of a situation in the past when you have given spoken instructions and the resulting action was **not** what you wanted. Perhaps the task was done badly, was not done at all or was done unwillingly.

Now jot down at least **three** examples when it was the way you gave the instructions which contributed to the poor result.

_____

_____

_____

_____

_____

_____

I have listed a number of examples from my own experience, perhaps your examples were similar. Mine were:

- I didn't think clearly in advance about what I wanted to say and was therefore very vague;

- I didn't check that they were listening properly before I started;

- I used technical terms that they didn't fully understand;

- I used words and a way of speaking that could have been misinterpreted;

- I used a tone of voice that was too aggressive or too weak;

- I didn't ask questions to see if they had understood properly.

When things go wrong we often find excuses for ourselves. A typical comment we have probably all made at some time is, 'I know what I said but what I meant was...' Therefore, whenever you are talking to people face-to-face or on the telephone, you need to remember a few basic points.

- **Prepare**
  You need to be clear in your own mind what you want to say **before** you say it. This will help to make the message **accurate** and **clear**.

- **Switch on the other person**
  Make sure the other person is **listening** before you start. You can do this very simply by asking a question. Alternatively you can make a statement such as, 'I'd like to talk to you about...'

- **Speak clearly and audibly**
  If you do, the listener won't have the embarrassment of having to ask you to repeat information.

- **Use familiar words and phrases**
  In this way there is less chance of being misunderstood. If new technical terms have to be used, make sure you explain them.

- **Use a tone of voice which suits the situation**
  The actual sound of your voice, combined with the words you choose, should convey the message accurately. For example, you would use a cheerful tone for good news, a more severe tone for a discipline interview.

- **Playback**
  Use questions to ensure that your listener can **repeat the message accurately** to you so you know that you have been understood correctly.

Finally remember that people are more willing to respond positively, particularly to instructions, if they know **why** they have to do something. After all, can you do a really good job if you don't know why you're doing it? Let's put some of the above points into practice in the next activity.

■ Time guide 5 minutes

A section supervisor in a bank is giving a new girl who is about to start work as a clerk some last minute instructions. He states: 'Finally, the bank demands that you look right'.

To what extent does this message fulfil the ABC of good communication?

Accurate _____

Brief _____

Clear _____

I hope you agree with my answer – 'Not very well!' For example:

■ Accurate
Is it the bank or the supervisor who is making the demands? Is 'demands' the right word? Does this mean that disciplinary action can be taken?

■ Brief
It is certainly brief – but at the expense of clarity. The message is incomplete. It does not provide sufficient detail.

■ Clear
The message is totally unclear. The words 'look right' are far too vague. Does this apply to dress? If so, what is the dress code the supervisor has in mind? Does it relate to other physical characteristics, such as hair?

Certainly this clerk will go away in a quandary unless she asks some questions! She'll probably go and ask other clerks what the supervisor meant. Let's start again with this scenario from the supervisor's viewpoint.

■ Preparation
The supervisor wants to convey the message that he likes female staff to wear simple, conservative clothes for work rather than high fashion and that hair should be clean and tidy.

■ Switch on
He could ask a question about clothes or make a comment such as, 'That's a very smart suit you're wearing. Why did you decide it was appropriate for working in a bank?'

■ Speak clearly and audibly
The supervisor would need to speak clearly and reasonably slowly to make sure the clerk hears every word.

■ Use familiar words and phrases
He should use normal conversational vocabulary. If he uses technical terms such as 'dress code', he also needs to explain that this is a set of simple rules about the type of clothes people are expected to wear to work at the bank.

■ Tone
The tone needs to be brisk, assertive but friendly. It should be brisk and assertive because he needs to convey that this is an essential part of the clerical job; friendly because he is advising a new employee, not reprimanding an existing member of his workteam for failing to obey the code.

■ Playback
He can finish by saying, 'I've told you something about how I and the bank like our clerks to look. Perhaps we better make sure we're in agreement. What kind of clothes do you think the bank would consider were unsuitable for work?'

■ Why
He should recognize that a new clerk would appreciate an explanation of why the dress code exists. The probable explanation is because clerks are visible to members of the public and the bank wants to convey a good public image of order and efficiency.

Now we have looked at some of the skills of speaking, let's turn to a set of skills which often accompany speaking in face-to-face situations, *behaving skills*.

6   Behaving skills

The third way in which we can communicate is by conveying a message through the way we look or behave. Very often we use behaviour to add weight to what we say. Try the following activity.

Activity 21

■ Time guide 5 minutes

Write down *three* forms of behaviour you can use to reinforce the spoken message, 'No – I don't agree with that!'

_____

_____

_____

See if your list is similar to mine. You can:

■ shake your head;

■ glare at the other person;

■ frown;

■ cross your arms firmly;

■ stamp your foot;

■ bang your fist.

This example shows that we use:

● *eye contact*;

● *facial expressions*;

● *gestures*;

● *stance and posture*

to convey a message. This non-verbal communication is often referred to as 'body language'. In the above activity body language confirmed the message being given. The next activity shows that this is not always the case.

Activity 22

■ Time guide 5 minutes

A member of your workteam has come to you with a suggestion for improving work methods.

Your words to her are: 'I think that's a very good idea. I'll certainly think very seriously about adopting it.'

Your body language is:

■ you avoid meeting her eyes;

■ you finger your collar;

■ you back away from her while speaking.

What message does that person actually receive from your behaviour?

_____

_____

My interpretation of the message was: 'I think that's a lousy idea and in no way am I going to use it.'

Did you agree? Our body language can sometimes let us down by conveying a totally different message from the spoken word. When body language contradicts speech, we often pay more attention to what we see than what we hear and respond to the behaviour rather than the words.

> Our behaviour speaks louder than our words.

This brings us to another important point about our behaviour. We can deliberately use body language to confirm what we are saying – **our behaviour is intentional**. However, a great deal of our body language may be unconscious – we are not aware of the non-verbal signals we are giving to other people. When we are caught in unguarded moments we may well communicate messages we do not intend other people to receive. There's an example of this below.

Case Study

John Olumide had been confident that he would be promoted to the post of supervisor in his section. When he was called into the office, he expected his manager to congratulate him. Instead, she told him that she was sorry but she was promoting an older member of the workteam who had more experience. John attempted to hide his disappointment and said: 'That's great! Jenny deserves it.'

However, as he said the words:

● *his shoulders slumped;*

● *the expectant broad smile on his face was replaced by one that was fixed;*

● *he avoided meeting her eyes.*

Unintentionally he had conveyed his disappointment through his body language.

This shows that quite frequently:

> we can send unintentional behavioural messages.

As a supervisor, you need to use body language intentionally and positively to help you in your job.

One problem that often worries newly appointed supervisors is whether they appear sufficiently assertive to their workteam so that they gain their co-operation and respect. Some may overdo assertiveness and show aggressive behaviour; others may lack confidence and show themselves to be rather weak. In the next activity we have shown some typical behavioural signals which convey this.

Activity 23

■ Time guide 8 minutes

For each type of behaviour listed, tick whether you would consider it a sign of aggression, assertiveness or weakness.

Behaviour	Aggressive	Assertive	Weak
Jabbing a finger at someone when giving an instruction			
Maintaining frequent eye contact when talking to a member of your workteam			
Sitting hunched over your desk and fiddling with your papers when disciplining a member of your workteam			
Leaning forward slightly and smiling at an applicant in a selection interview			
Drumming your fingers on the desk while explaining a technical detail.			

I thought that aggressive behaviour was shown by:

■ jabbing a finger;

■ drumming your fingers on the desk.

Weak behaviour was shown by:

■ sitting hunched over your desk;

■ fiddling with papers.

Assertive behaviour was shown by:

■ frequent eye contact;

■ leaning forward slightly and smiling.

You need to adopt assertive behaviour. Here are some examples of positive body language, which you can use to show assertiveness in a variety of situations.

● *Frequent eye contact*
  Your can use your eyes to establish contact, develop a rapport and show interest.

● *A range of facial expressions*

Your should allow your face to support your message. This means displaying a whole range of emotions through the way that you look. An aggressive person will look constantly bad-tempered while a weak person will always look anxious.

● *Upright but relaxed posture*

This applies whether standing or sitting. Good posture actually conveys confidence, alertness and interest as well as helping you to breathe and speak more easily.

● *Open gestures*

You will find that assertiveness can be conveyed through certain gestures. For example, use a firm handshake when greeting people. If you are using your hands when explaining a point, then use them with the palms upwards to show sincerity and honesty.

Body language can be a useful aid in communicating to your workteam. Another form of behaviour that can act as a form of communication to your workteam is the way you carry out your own work. Bad attitudes to work can quickly be communicated to other people and then influence their own behaviour, as in the example below.

Frank was the supervisor in the order processing section. Despite being a 'tough' supervisor, his workteam had the worst attendance record in the department and an increasing number of errors were found in their orders. Frank blamed his workteam for shoddy work.

In one exit interview with a clerk who was leaving, it came to light that the team had stopped caring about their work because Frank did't seem to worry about anything except the number of orders they processed. He took long tea breaks and frequently wandered off to other sections while they were working.

The team had taken their lead from Frank. He had set them a bad example and they had followed it.

Setting a good example is a form of behavioural communication.

So far, we have considered our personal behaviour as part of behavioural communication. There is one other form of behavioural communication which is conveyed by the **symbols that surround our jobs**.

Activity 24

■ Time guide 2 minutes

Joel Webley was appointed supervisor of the porters after three years at Denwitch Hospital. The first morning in his new job, he turned up in the porters' room and chatted to the men as usual while they all got ready for work. When they saw Joel in his white uniform it reminded them that Joel was now the supervisor.

Which of the following reasons do you think accounts for this?

■ He'd taken the overalls home and washed them.

■ The overalls were brand new.

■ White overalls were his badge of office.

The last reason is the most likely. Some of you, like Joel, may wear different colour overalls to distinguish you from members of your workteam – uniforms are a common form of behavioural communication. They tell people about authority and status.

Activity 25

Part B

■ Time guide 5 minutes

Try to identify *two* other symbols which surround your own job that convey messages about your authority and status.

_____

_____

_____

_____

Your might have thought of more than two. I have chosen some typical status symbols in my list. These are:

■ a personalized parking space in the car park;

■ a different kind of desk or chair;

■ whether you have to clock on for work;

■ the canteen in which you eat.

You may not be able to control this kind of behavioural message – it goes with the job – but it is just as well to be aware that it exists!

Now you are ready to think about developing your own behavioural communication skills. In doing this you should:

● Think about the impact of your body language on others;

● Use behaviour that reinforces your words to ensure the right action.

This part of the unit has looked at the skills you use as a sender when communicating. The next part will consider the main skill needed by receivers – the ability to *listen*.

Self check 2

■ Time guide 5 minutes

Complete the following sentences with a suitable word or words.

1. Effective communication means being accurate, _____ and _____ .

2. It is important to think carefully about your written communication because it is projecting an image of _____ .

3. The way you see eye contact, facial expressions, gestures and posture is often referred to as _____ _____ .

4. Setting a good example is a form of _____ communication.

5. Select the *two* correct words from the list below.

   Communication should be:

   (a) clear;

   (b) complacent;

   (c) complex;

   (d) concise.

37

Response check 2

1. Effective communication means being accurate, BRIEF and CLEAR.

2. It is important to think carefully about your written communication because it is projecting an image of YOU.

3. The way you see eye contact, facial expressions, gestures, posture is often referred to as BODY LANGUAGE.

4. Setting a good example is a form of BEHAVIOURAL communication.

5. (a) clear and (d) concise are CORRECT.

   (b) complacent is INCORRECT because it means self-righteous or smug and we should never be this when communicating.

   (c) complex is INCORRECT because it means complicated. We want to communicate in a simple, straightforward way so that other people understand us correctly.

---

7   Summary

Whenever you speak or write, remember the basic principles of communication:

● accuracy;

● brevity;

● clarity;

● clear communication;

● complete communication;

● concise communication;

● correct communication;

● courteous communication.

You should select a method of communication that is suited to any situation bearing in mind:

● clarity;

● speed;

● cost effectiveness;

● attitude of receiver.

It is important to remember that:

● every piece of writing is projecting an image of you.

In order to convey a written message that is understood and acted upon:

● keep your reader in the forefront of your mind.

In speaking to others:

● engage brain before opening mouth.

In order to convey a spoken message well:

● prepare;

● switch on the listener;

● speak clearly and audibly;

● use familiar words and phrases;

● use a tone which reflects the message;

● ask for playback.

Behavioural messages can be conveyed through:

● eye contact;

● facial expression;

● gestures;

● stance and posture.

Remember that where there is a contradiction between speech and behaviour:

● behaviour speaks louder than words.

Develop body language which is:

● positive;

● intentional.

THE SKILL OF LISTENING

1   Introduction

Supervisors need to be competent as senders in the communication process; they also need to be effective receivers. Information, instructions, advice and requests will come from the workteam, management and other sections and you have a responsibility to *listen*. Listening is the key to understanding and taking appropriate action.

Let's begin by looking at the importance of listening skills and then investigate how we often allow ourselves to be poor listeners. Finally, there are some practical points on how you can improve you own listening skills.

Extension 2 If you want to find out more about how to develop your listening skills, you will find useful information in this extension.

2   The importance of listening

In your job, you probably find that you spend a high proportion of your time writing and talking to people. However, do you spend enough time listening? It was pointed out in a training course on communication skills that: 'Perhaps we have been given two ears and only one mouth for a purpose – so that we can listen twice as much as we speak!' There is a strong element of truth in this humerous remark.

Activity 26

■ Time guide 6 minutes

Why do you think it is necessary to be a good listener in your role as a supervisor? Try to jot down *three* reasons.

_____

_____

_____

I hope we can agree that listening is a vital skill at work. See if your reasons are similar to mine. Listening enables you to:

■ act on instructions and advice quickly and accurately;

■ pick up good ideas from other people;

■ discover why members of your workteam hold certain attitudes towards you and their work;

■ be more approachable as a leader of your workteam when dealing with complaints, problems, etc.

The two-way communication process cannot be effective unless you listen, understand and act. In other words, you cannot do your job properly unless you are prepared to listen carefully.

Listening is an essential part of the communication process.

I'm sure you have recognized this as good common sense; it is surprising how easy it is for us to lapse into being poor listeners.

3	Barriers to effective listening

One of the basic reasons for poor listening is our own attitude to this activity. We tend to consider it an automatic process. If someone is speaking, because we hear the words, we assume we are listening. This is not always the case. We should never confuse *hearing* with *listening*. Hearing is a *passive* experience. Hearing is expecting our ears to do all the work. Listening involves the mind actually using its existing knowledge to make sense of the new information. It is hearing and interpreting information so that we understand and act correctly.

Listening is an active process.

When we view listening as a passive experience we fall prey to a number of practices which interfere with our ability to listen.

Activity 27

> ■ **Time guide 6 minutes**
>
> **Think back to an occasion when you were being briefed by your manager or were sitting in a meeting and you were conscious that your were not listening properly.**
>
> **What affected your ability to listen?**
>
> _____
>
> _____
>
> _____
>
> _____

In your answer, have you blamed the speaker or yourself?

Of course there are some speakers that make it very difficult for their listeners – they are inaudible, muddled or vague. However, most of the fault lies with the listener. For example, as a listener you may:

● become absorbed in noticing *distracting features about the speaker* rather than concentrating on the substance of the message. For example, you may be distracted by a physical characteristic or a mannerism;

● allow *distractions in your environment* to disturb your concentration too easily, this may be someone walking past, the ringing of a telephone or the behaviour of other people in the room;

● fail to look at the speaker so that you *miss the behavioural signals* which help you to understand the message;

● *'switch off' deliberately* because you have taken offence at the tone of the speaker or reacted emotionally to a phrase he or she has used;

- allow existing **negative attitudes towards the speaker** to block your concentration;
- try to **do two things at once** such as trying to write a memo at the same time as listening to an instruction.

We can summarize these various faults by saying that listeners can often be distracted from the substance of the message by:

- the **speaker;**
- their **environment;**
- their own **feelings** and **attitudes**.

Once you recognize these are common faults to which we all succumb and admit that you can be guilty of them too, you are half-way to improving your listening skills.

4 Characteristics of good listeners

There are some practical steps you can take to improve your own listening skills. These all lie within your control. The next activity encourages you to identify some of the characteristics of good listeners from your own observation or experience.

Activity 28

■ Time guide 5 minutes

Write down **three** things that good listeners do.

One example is that they concentrate on the **substance** of the message.

_____

_____

_____

Here is a list of things that good listeners tend to do.

■ Keep their eyes focused on the speaker.

This enables them to interpret the body language as well as listen to the words.

■ Let the sender make his or her points.

They don't interrupt unnecessarily.

■ Demonstrate that they are listening.

They use simple phrases, words or noises that show that they are giving the words their attention while not interrupting the speaker. Some examples are 'I see', 'OK', 'Umm' or show their attention by their body language.

■ Concentrate on key phrases, stressed words.

By doing this they can extract the essential information from surrounding detail.

■ Write down brief notes.

This enables them to make sure they have the key facts correct, particularly if the message is long, complex or involves detailed instructions.

■ Ask questions.

Questions allow them to clear up misunderstandings and to find out any additional information they need.

■ Offer feedback.

This enables them to show that they have understood the message correctly and are prepared to act.

If you can use these simple techniques yourself, they will make you a more effective listener in face-to-face situations. Listening is a much easier activity when sender and receiver can see one another. This is because you employ body language as a listener just as much as you do as a speaker.

Below is a list of some of the ways in which you can show that you are listening.

● Meeting the eye of the sender.

● Your facial expressions.

Your facial expressions can show doubt, anxiety, pleasure.

● Using appropriate gestures.

You can nod your head in agreement, shake your head in disagreement, stroke your chin to show that you are evaluating an idea.

● Using posture to demonstrate attention.

You can show concentration by sitting quietly and still and by leaning slightly forward towards the speaker.

Telephone conversations are more difficult because there is no body language to help you.

Activity 29

■ Time guide 5 minutes

What techniques can you use in your telephone conversation to demonstrate that you are listening actively to the other person? Jot down *one* or *two* ideas.

_____

_____

Now see if your ideas are similar to those I thought of. You could:

■ use 'Yes', 'I see' when the sender is giving detailed information and a longer reply might distract them;

■ ask follow-up questions on the information given, which show that you have received and understood the message;

■ repeat key facts: times, dates, numbers.

As you can see, on the telephone your other communication skills must compensate for the absence of body language.

You might also like to test your own concentration by listening to a news bulletin on the radio and then recalling all the news items in the right order. You will need to tape the bulletin as well to check whether you were correct.

One of the benefits of being a good listener is that it tends to improve other people's communication skills. Public speakers will tell you that an attentive, interested audience can really help them to improve their own delivery. The rapport has been established. The same is true at work. If you can show yourself to be a good listener, you will often help other people to speak more clearly and accurately.

5   Listening to behaviour

So far, we have used the word 'listening' as a process involving the ears and the brain. A good dictionary would also explain listening as 'paying attention to'. We are going to use the word in this context in this last section. Supervisors need to *pay attention to behavioural messages* from their workteam.

Marked changes in behaviour, particularly a fall in performance, are often signs that someone has a problem. We need to be able to spot these signals as soon as possible and respond to them.

Imagine, for example, that a pleasant, punctual, hardworking machinist changes overnight – she arrives late on two consecutive days, is surly and becomes increasingly careless in her work. If you are 'listening' to her behaviour it should tell you that something is wrong and that as the supervisor you must deal with this problem.

Other behavioural symptoms that supervisors need to note are *aggressiveness* or *defensiveness* in members of their workteam. Where these occur, the underlying cause could be that the person feels threatened or under some kind of stress. Too often we can dismiss this type of behaviour as someone 'going through a rough patch' or 'in one of their moods' and pay very little attention to it. Paying heed to behavioural communication is the first step to solving the problem. Failing to take notice of these signals will only allow the situation to get worse. It is therefore important that you:

> pay attention to behaviour as well as words.

Let's now look at these ideas in a practical situation in the following incident.

Part C

Activity 30

■ Time guide 5 minutes

Harry Wrath is a skilled lathe operator. About six months ago the company for which he then worked made half the workforce redundant to new technology. Harry was one of those to go. Fortunately he got a new job quickly and settled in well – he enjoyed working for his new firm.

*After four months he and others were informed by their supervisor that the firm was to introduce computer assisted machines which were needed for the firm to remain competitive. The supervisor made it clear that Harry and the others **would not lose their jobs**. Privately the supervisor considered it would benefit them in terms of increased pay and improved working conditions.*

Harry's attitude to his work began to deteriorate. His supervisor found him surly and difficult to handle. Harry tried to persuade the union branch to oppose the introduction of the new technology. When this wasn't accepted Harry became even more difficult. He became argumentative and unpleasant.

Do you believe Harry's aggressiveness is due to his past experience of new technology?

Yes	No

If you were Harry's supervisor would you

■ Ignore his behaviour?

■ Tell him to pull himself together?

■ Talk to him about his opposition?

■ Report him to your manager?

I think you'll agree that the answer to the first question is *yes*. Harry lost his last job when new technology was introduced and this is obviously still on his mind.

The most useful action you can take is 'talk to him about his opposition'. You must listen to him to find out fully why his opposition is so strong and then use your own knowledge about the details of the new technology to be introduced to show him how it will help him, rather than deprive him of his job. Only a full and frank exchange of information is likely to help his behaviour return to normal.

One way to develop your ability to 'listen to behaviour' and to interpret other people's body language is to watch a silent film such as one starring Charlie Chaplin or Laurel and Hardy; alternatively, you could watch television with the sound turned right down. This will sharpen your powers of observation very quickly.

Effective communication is not always easy but when the process is successful it does make the work of a supervisor more productive and less frustrating.

■ Time guide 5 minutes

Which of the following statements are TRUE and which are FALSE?

1. Hearing is the same as listening. TRUE/FALSE

2. Poor listening is the fault of the speaker. TRUE/FALSE

3. Good listeners demonstrate they are listening. TRUE/FALSE

4. You should pay attention to behaviour as well as listening to words when communicating with your workteam. TRUE/FALSE

Complete the following sentences with a suitable word or words.

6. Listeners can be distracted from the _____ of the message by the speaker, their _____ or their own feelings and attitudes.

7. Listening is an _____ process.

8. Good listeners focus their eyes on the _____.

9. Behavioural symptoms that a member of your workteam may be under pressure are aggressiveness and _____.

Response check 3

1. Hearing is the same as listening. This is FALSE. Hearing is a matter of receiving a cluster of words with your ears. Listening is a totally active process which involves the brain in interpreting the words to form a message.

2. Poor listening is the fault of the speaker. This is FALSE. A listener should never blame a speaker for his or her own inability to concentrate properly.

3. Good listeners demonstrate they are listening. This is TRUE.

4. You should pay attention to behaviour as well as listen to words when communicating with your workteam. This is TRUE.

5. Listeners can be distracted from the SUBSTANCE (or content) of the message by the speaker, their ENVIRONMENT (or surroundings) and their own attitudes and feelings.

6. Listening is an ACTIVE process.

7. Good listeners focus their eyes on the SPEAKER.

8. Behavioural symptoms that a member of your workteam is under pressure are aggressiveness and DEFENSIVENESS.

- Listening is an essential part of the communication process.
- Hearing is not the same as listening.
- You can't help hearing: listening needs thinking about.

Most listening faults are because the listener becomes distracted by:

- the speaker;
- their environment;
- their own attitudes and feelings.

The characteristics of good listeners are that they:

- focus their eyes on the speaker;
- let the sender make his or her points;
- demonstrate they are listening;
- concentrate on key phrases and stressed words;
- write down brief notes;
- ask questions;
- offer feedback.

A good supervisor also:

- pays attention to behaviour as well as words, particularly changes in behaviour.

1   Quick quiz

Well done – you have completed the text part of the unit. Now listen to the questions on Side one of the audio cassette. If you are not sure about some of the answers, check back in the workbook before making up your mind.

Write down your answers in the space below.

1 _____

_____

2 _____

_____

3 _____

_____

4 _____

_____

5 _____

_____

6 _____

_____

7 _____

_____

8 _____

_____

9 _____

_____

10 _____

_____

11 _____

_____

12 _____

_____

13 _____

_____

14 _____

_____

15 _____

_____

2   Action check

On Side two of the audio cassette you will hear some extracts from conversations about communication. Listen carefully to the extracts and then try to answer the questions.

Write your answers and comments in the space below.

Situation 1:

_____

_____

_____

_____

_____

_____

Situation 2:

_____

_____

_____

_____

_____

Situation 3:

_____

_____

_____

_____

_____

_____

_____

_____

_____

_____

---

3   Unit assessment

Time guide 60 minutes

Read the following case incident and then deal with the questions which follow, writing your answers on a separate sheet of paper.

The past year had been a little unsettled at Kay's Castings. During the year a number of rumours had arisen about the company's future. One rumour hinted of an expansion of the labour force, only to be followed shortly after by another about redundancy. The latest rumour, which arose from the current wage negotiations, suggested that Kay's was to be taken over by a larger group of companies. This rumour was denied by Kay's management as quite ill-founded.

For several weeks the personnel office had been preparing for a visit by a group of City stockbrokers. These visits were quite common and helped the 'City' to keep in touch with companies in whose shares they were dealing.

There was nothing sinister in the visit, but rumours soon began to get around. On the day of the visit Kay's directors were out in force – each of them showed their group of visitors round the factory.

Paul Dunn was a long-serving and loyal member of the workforce – he was also one of the trade union shop stewards. He normally acted very sensibly and calmly, but on the day of the visit he acted very aggressively. Although he had been informed about the purpose of the visit, he stormed into his manager's office, 'What's really going on with this visit? I asked a couple of them what they are here for and couldn't get any sense out of them!'

Jim Dale, the manager, was already having an anxious time keeping production going whilst at the same time attempting to impress his directors and visitors. His reply was quite short, 'Look Paul, you were told six weeks ago what the visit was for. These people can make or break a company like ours. The last thing they want to see is your machine idle – so why not get back to your job and leave me to get on with mine'.

Paul returned to his machine angry and worried. When tea break came Paul took the opportunity to work off his anger at Jim and the visitors by grumbling to his mates. After a while the whole section was angry and worried. The result was that whenever the opportunity arose, they stood around and angrily talked with each other. A lot of this took place around the doors of the washroom and had also begun to interfere with the access to Jim Dale's office.

You only need to write *one* or *two* sentences against each question.

1. List *two* likely causes of the rumours.

2. Why does Paul Dunn deserve better treatment from his manager than he actually received?

3. Show how our four-point planning approach *what*, *who*, *how*, *why* would have improved Jim Dale's communication with Paul Dunn.

4. What was the feedback that Jim Dale appeared to ignore?

4 Work-based assignment

Time guide 60 minutes

The time guide for this assignment gives you an approximate idea of how long it is likely to take you to write up your findings.

You will need to spend some additional time gathering information, perhaps talking to colleagues and thinking about the assignment. The result of your efforts should be presented on separate sheets of paper.

Recall two communication situations in which you or a colleague have been involved. You should choose one example of an effective communication and one example where communication went wrong.

Analyse each situation using our communication model. It is repeated here to remind you.

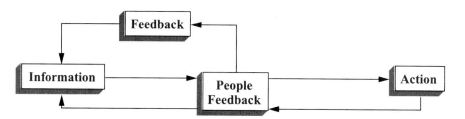

In your analysis you should describe each stage and how why one communication was effective and why the other failed.

UNIT REVIEW

1 Return to objectives

Now that you have completed your work on this unit, let's review each of our unit objectives.

You should be *better able to*:

● identify the benefits to you of being a good communicator;

Communication is essential to good management, therefore understanding what is involved in the communication process and using that process more effectively will enable you to be a better leader, planner, organizer and co-ordinator.

● design your communication to achieve the results you want;

After reading about the communication process and some of the techniques of writing, speaking and behaving, you should be able to plan your communication to convey information accurately, briefly and clearly to your workteam, and secure feedback from them so that you can be certain they will act on the information in the correct way.

● communicate more effectively in speech, writing and behaviour;

You can use the ABC and five Cs of communication as a simple guide for all your communication. If you adopt the suggestions made in the sections on writing, speaking and behaving and carry out your action plan, you will find that your own communication will continue to improve.

● listen effectively.

Now you are aware of how and why we tend to be poor listeners, you can adopt a more positive and active approach to listening to words and behaviour so that you can provide accurate person and action feedback to others.

2 Extensions

Extension 1

Video: *In Charge*

Distributor: The Open College

Programme 1 of this video will help you to appreciate the importance of communicating well and the part communication plays in being an effective supervisor.

Extension 2

Book: *What Do You Mean 'Communication'?* An introduction to communication in business

Author: N. Stanton

Publisher: Pan Breakthrough Books

This book expands on all aspects covered in this unit. It is written in a readable style and you should find Chapter 1 on breakdown in communication; Chapter 2 on understanding the communication process; Chapter 7 on listening and Chapters 10 and 11 on preparing and planning to communicate particularly helpful.

Extension 3

Video: *A Question of May*

Distributor: Rank Training

This short video demonstrates well the usefulness of our communication model. It also covers barriers to communication and suggests ways of overcoming them.

Extension 4

Book: *Business Communication Made Simple*

Author: E. C. Eyre

Publisher: Heinemann

This book provides short chapters on most aspects of business communication. In particular, you should find that Chapter 6 on methods of communication; Chapter 17 on aspects of written language and Chapter 20 on verbal communication are well worth reading.

These Extensions and videos can be taken up via your Support Centre. They will arrange that you have access to them. However, it may be more convenient to check out the materials with your own personnel or training people at work – they could well give you access. There are other good reasons for approaching your own people as, by doing so, they will become aware of your continuing interest in the subject and you will be able to involve them in your development.

ACTION PLAN

Work out your own plan of action for improving the communication skills of your team by responding to the following check questions and picking up the ■ action prompts.

Check questions

Your response and intended action:

1 What do you want to achieve through improving your communications at work?

_____

_____

_____

■ *State your personal objectives clearly.*

2 Which of the basic skills needs most attention?

_____

_____

_____

■ *Decide the priority and how you will allocate your time to improve your various skills.*

3 What kind of information do you have to convey at work?

_____

_____

_____

■ *Identify the different kinds of information you have to convey and decide whether you are using the most appropriate methods.*

4 What kind of people make up your workteam? How can you use this information about them in your communication?

_____

_____

_____

■ *Consider each individual's attitudes and knowledge in deciding how to convey messages to them.*

5 How can you get feedback from your workteam?

_____

_____

_____

■ *Devise some techniques for getting your workteam to playback instructions.*

6 What kind of image of you does your own written communication convey?

_____

_____

_____

■ *Take a long, critical look at a range of written communication and identify anything that conveys a poor image of you.*

7 Do you always
follow the basic
points identified
in the section on
speaking skills?

_____

_____

_____

■ *If not, identify which points you need to concentrate upon and put
these into practice.*

8 Do you use any body
language which is
over-aggressive or
weak when
communicating?

_____

_____

_____

■ *Find out from others (at work or home) and work hard at
developing assertive body language.*

9 Do you set a good
example to your
workteam? If not,
why not?

_____

_____

_____

■ *If not, try to pinpoint what aspects of your behaviour may not set a
good example and work on improving this behaviour.*

10 Do you listen well?

_____

_____

_____

■ *If not, identify what distractors influence you and work hard at
using the concentration techniques mentioned in Part C.*

Now you have produced an action plan, you should note that you
cannot put all ten actions into effect at the same time.

■ ***prioritize*** your ten actions;

■ give yourself specific ***time deadlines*** for achieving them.